The Great Seal of the United States

by Norman Pearl

illustrated by Matthew Skeens

PICTURE WINDOW BOOKS
Minneapolis, Minnesota

Special thanks to our advisers for their expertise:

Kevin Byrne, Ph.D., Professor of History
Gustavus Adolphus College

Susan Kesselring, M.A., Literacy Educator
Rosemount-Apple Valley-Eagan (Minnesota) School District

Editor: Jill Kalz
Designer: Nathan Gassman
Page Production: Ellen Schofield
Creative Director: Keith Griffin
Editorial Director: Carol Jones
The illustrations in this book were created digitally.

Picture Window Books
1710 Roe Crest Drive
North Mankato, MN 56003-0669
877-845-8392
www.capstonepub.com

Library of Congress Cataloging-in-Publication Data
Pearl, Norman.
The great seal of the United States / by Norman Pearl ; illustrated by Matthew Skeens.
p. cm. — (American symbols)
Includes bibliographical references and index.
ISBN-13: 978-1-4048-2214-6 (hardcover)
ISBN-13: 978-1-4048-2220-7 (paperback)
1. United States—Seal—Juvenile literature. 2. Bald eagle—Juvenile literature. 3. Signs and
symbols—United States—Juvenile literature. I. Skeens, Matthew. II. Title.
III. American symbols (Picture Window Books)
CD5610.P43 2007
929.9—dc22   2006003374

Table of Contents

My name is Benjamin Franklin.
I helped make the first laws of the United
States more than 200 years ago. I also
helped design the Great Seal. The
Great Seal is a symbol of the
United States and the U.S.
government. Let me tell
you more about it!

What Is the Great Seal?

The Great Seal is a special mark. It is put on important government papers. People know that any paper with the Great Seal on it is from the U.S. government.

No one except the U.S. government is allowed to use the Great Seal.

A Country Is Born

The story of the Great Seal starts on July 4, 1776. That's when the Declaration of Independence was approved, and the United States of America was born.

The new country needed to set itself apart from other countries. The United States needed its own seal. A committee was formed to design one.

Three Committees, Three Designs

The first design committee included Thomas Jefferson, John Adams, and me, Benjamin Franklin. We all had different ideas about what the seal should look like.

Congress had its own ideas, too. During the next six years, two more committees tried to create a seal. No one could find the perfect design.

Second Committee

Third Committee

Thomas Jefferson and John Adams had a lot in common. Both loved their country. Both signed the Declaration of Independence. Both later became President of the United States. And both died on July 4, 1826.

The Finished Product

Congress decided to give the seal project to Charles Thomson, the Secretary of Congress. Thomson looked at the ideas of all three committees. He asked a lawyer named William Barton to help him put the ideas together. Just seven days later, on June 20, 1782, Congress approved their design.

In 1782, seals were two-sided wax disks. They had one design on the front and one on the back. Later, seals were pressed into paper. Only the front design appeared. Today, only the front of the Great Seal is pressed into important U.S. government papers.

The Great Seal's Front

All of the objects and words on the Great Seal of the United States mean something. Do you see the bald eagle on the front? Thomson and Barton chose a North American bird because the seal is a symbol of a North American country.

The eagle has a shield with 13 red and white stripes. The number 13 appears many times on the Great Seal. It stands for the first 13 states of the United States. Above the stripes is a blue band. It stands for Congress.

The eagle has a ribbon in its beak. On the ribbon are the Latin words *E Pluribus Unum*. In English, these words mean "out of many, one." The words say that the many U.S. states came together as one strong country.

The eagle holds an olive branch in one claw. The branch is a symbol of peace. In its other claw, the eagle holds 13 arrows. The arrows show that Americans will fight to stay free.

Above the eagle are 13 stars in a ring of light. The stars stand for the United States taking its place among the other great countries of the world.

The Great Seal's Back

On the back of the Great Seal is an unfinished pyramid. It has 13 steps. The pyramid is a symbol of the United States' long-lasting strength.

ANNUIT COEPTIS

MDCCLXXVI

The eye is called the Eye of Providence. Above it are the Latin words *Annuit Coeptis*. In English, these words mean "He [God] has favored our undertakings." Together, the eye and the words suggest that the United States has a bright future.

At the bottom of the pyramid are some Roman numerals, or numbers: MDCCLXXVI. They stand for "1776." The Latin words *Novus Ordo Seclorum* mean "new order of the ages." Together, the date and the words are symbols for the birth of the United States in 1776.

CCLXXVI

19

Seeing the Great Seal

The Great Seal appears on many important U.S. government papers. For example, the Great Seal is put on treaties. Treaties are agreements with other countries.

The tool used to press the Great Seal into government papers is in Washington, D.C. It sits in the Exhibit Hall of the State Department. Because the Great Seal is a valued symbol of the United States, this tool is well guarded.

Now you know the story of the Great Seal of the United States. Look for the seal the next time someone gives you a dollar bill. See if you can find all of the symbols you just read about!

Great Seal Facts

The Great Seal of
the United States

(front)

(back)

 Kings and other rulers have used seals for more than 6,000 years.

 Charles Thomson did not show any artwork to Congress. Members approved his design for the Great Seal from a written description.

 The bald eagle is not really bald. It has white feathers on its head. *Bald* is an old word for "white."

 The Great Seal is used on important U.S. government papers between 2,000 and 3,000 times a year.

 The Secretary of State is in charge of the Great Seal. Thomas Jefferson was the first Secretary of State of the United States and the first to take on this duty.

Glossary

approved — given the OK

committee — a group of people chosen for a special task

Congress — the group of people in the U.S. government who make laws

Declaration of Independence — the paper in which the American colonies said they were free from Great Britain; the Colonies later became the United States of America

design — to make something with a plan in mind

pyramid — an object with four triangle-shaped sides that meet at a point on top

seal — a mark or stamp

shield — a piece of armor used to protect the body from attack

symbol — an object that stands for something else

To Learn More

At the Library

Bateman, Teresa. *Red, White, Blue and Uncle Who?* New York: Holiday House, 2001.

DeGezelle, Terri. *The Great Seal of the United States.* Mankato, Minn.: Capstone Press, 2004.

On the Web

FactHound offers a safe, fun way to find Web sites related to this book. All of the sites on FactHound have been researched by our staff.

1. Visit *www.facthound.com*
2. Type in this special code: 1404822143
3. Click on the FETCH IT button.

Your trusty FactHound will fetch the best sites for you!

Index

Look for all of the books in the American Symbols series:

The Great Seal of the United States
1-4048-2214-3
Our American Flag
1-4048-2212-7
Our National Anthem
1-4048-2215-1
The Statue of Liberty
1-4048-2216-X
The U.S. Constitution
1-4048-2643-2
The White House
1-4048-2217-8